The Land and Peoples of
FRANCE

Ed Needham

A Watts Book

INTRODUCTION

Salut! We all come from France. We want to tell you about the history and geography of our country, the areas we live in, and some of the traditions and customs of the French people.

We are all French, we speak the same language and study the same subjects at school, but we come from different parts of the country, with various backgrounds and experiences to tell you about.

As you'll see, France is a country which is changing rapidly. Our parents didn't have computers or take holidays abroad. Some of our families were not living in this country twenty years ago. We all think of ourselves as French children, but we sometimes feel that we are not given the same rights and opportunities.

Carnac

Gwenaëlle is from Brittany where her family have lived for generations.

Simon is from Toulouse, a major industrial city.

Thierry is from the Basque country where regional culture is very strong.

Saint-Jean-de-Luz

• Toulouse

Sandrine is from Alsace, one of the famous wine-producing areas.

• Paris

Bernard is from Paris. His father works at the Louvre museum.

Kaysersberg •

Minh is from Lyon. Her grandparents came to France from Vietnam in the 1950s.

Lyon •

Kader is from Marseille. His parents moved to France from Algeria, twenty years ago.

Marseille •

CONTENTS

3

WELCOME TO FRANCE

France is roughly hexagonal in shape, and shares borders with Spain, Italy, Switzerland, Germany, Belgium, Luxembourg and Andorra. It is separated from Britain by the English Channel, called *La Manche*, or the sleeve, in French. Corsica, an island in the Mediterranean, is also part of France, as are Martinique, Guadeloupe in the Caribbean, French Guiana in South America and Réunion in the Indian Ocean.

France covers an area of 543,965 km^2, and has a population of nearly 57 million, 4.5 million of whom are originally from other countries. Its central position in Europe has helped make it a major trading nation. It is technologically advanced and has influence on European and world events. It plays a leading role in the European Union and the United Nations.

French landscape can be outstanding, such as that in Languedoc (right). The national language is, of course, French. The French word for country is *pays*, but many people also call their region, or area, their *pays* (opposite). They sometimes speak a second, regional language or dialect, such as Basque, Provençal or Breton.

ENGLAND

English Channel

Calais

NORD
PAS-DE-
CALAIS

Lille

BELGIUM

LUXEMBOURG

Brest

Somme

UPPER
NORMANDY

PICARDY

GERMANY

BRITTANY

LOWER
NORMANDY

Oise

Paris

ILE DE FRANCE

Marne

Seine

LORRAINE

ALSACE

Strasbourg

Loire

CHAMPAGNE-ARDENNE

Marne-Saône Canal

PAYS DE LA LOIRE

CENTRE

BURGUNDY

Bay of
Biscay

Vienne

FRANCE

Loire

Saône

FRANCHE-COMTE

SWITZERLAND

POITOU
CHARENTES

Allier

Lake Geneva

Bordeaux

LIMOUSIN

Dordogne

Lyon

AUVERGNE

Garonne

RHONE-ALPES

AQUITAINE

Rhône

ITALY

Toulouse

MIDI-PYRENEES

SPAIN

LANGUEDOC-ROUSSILLON

PROVENCE-ALPES-
COTE D'AZUR

ANDORRA

Marseille

Nice

Mediterranean Sea

CORSICA

PEOPLE

Over the centuries, waves of migrating and invading people have settled in France. When Julius Caesar invaded in 58 BC, France covered roughly the same area as today, although the Romans called it Gaul. The French language is a mixture of Latin, which the Romans spoke, and the language of the ancient peoples known as the Celts. After the Romans came the Franks. They were a Germanic tribe, who gave France its name and created a powerful Christian kingdom.

The many battles and occupations of France has increased the mix of people living here. Muslims from North Africa briefly occupied south-western France, and for many centuries our country has had a large Jewish population.

More recently, people have left their own countries and settled in France to escape persecution and war. Others have come from lands that France controlled in the past (known as colonies), such as Algeria in North Africa, in search of a higher standard of living. Still more have moved to France from other European countries.

Charlemagne (right) became king of the Franks in 771 AD. He conquered much of western Europe, and united it in one great empire.

Today, most of France's old colonies govern themselves, but some still have close ties with France. People from North and West Africa (left) and South-East Asia have moved to France and become French citizens, but they often choose to keep their culture intact. Obtaining legal entry into France can be difficult because of the government's concern about overcrowding. Those who enter a foreign country to live are called immigrants (above).

Gwenaëlle lives near Carnac in Brittany. We know that people have lived in this area for thousands of years, because of the ancient megaliths (stone monuments) that remain in the landscape (left). The Bretons are descended from the Celts, as were the Irish, Scots and Welsh. Their language, Breton, is linked to Welsh and Cornish.

LANDSCAPE AND REGIONS

Gwenaëlle lives in Brittany, on the Atlantic coast in north-western France. Brittany is green and wet, cold in winter but pleasant in summer, with a rugged coastline and dramatic sea. It has many pretty fishing villages, dairy farms and fashionable resorts.

Down in the south lies the Côte d'Azur, the Blue Coast (left), which is on the Mediterranean, near the Italian border. Here, the sandy beaches attract thousands of tourists during the baking hot summers. Inland, vineyards, citrus trees and lavender fields colour the landscape.

Some of us spend our winter holidays skiing in the Alps, further north. Mont Blanc in the Alps (far left) is the highest mountain in Europe, at 4,807 m. Another mountain range, the Pyrenees, separates France from Spain, and in the centre of the country is a huge mountainous area called the Massif Central. The most important rivers are the Seine, the Loire, the Rhône and the Garonne.

France has lush green fields and rolling hills (left), orchards, vineyards, snowy mountains, wild coastlines and sunny beaches. It is rare to find so many variations of landscape and climate in a single country.

FOOD AND SHOPPING

The French take their food very seriously – the quality of the ingredients is essential and meal times are important occasions.

France has a long tradition of producing some of the world's greatest chefs and most sophisticated dishes, but even basic items, such as bread, wine or cheese, are expected to be made to very high standards.

Every French town and village has shops such as the *boulangerie* (bakery), *pâtisserie* (cake and sweet shop) and *charcuterie* (pork butchers), but typical dishes vary between areas, depending on local produce. *Bouillabaisse*, a fish stew, is from Marseille, while *escargots*, or snails cooked in parsley and garlic, is typical of Burgundy.

In the cities it is possible to find food from around the world. Immigrants enjoy eating their traditional dishes, which are also popular with other French people, so there are shops selling ingredients for Algerian, Vietnamese or Italian recipes.

The French enjoy shopping for food as well as eating it; open-air markets are a common sight in every town. The photograph shows a stall selling garlic.

Kader's parents are from Algeria, in North Africa. With his family, he might eat dishes such as *couscous*, a type of steamed grain, with lamb or chicken, and vegetables such as courgettes and chick peas; *chorba*, a vegetable soup; or *makrot*, which is semolina with almonds (above). This might be followed by strong, black coffee. Cold meats and seasoned sausages are popular in France (top right), as are shellfish delicacies (right), throughout the country.

11

 Some Jews go to the synagogue everyday, but Simon only goes on Saturday, with his family. The service is led by a rabbi (left). Once a week he goes to classes to learn about the Jewish prophets and to read and write Hebrew script. The Cathedral of Notre Dame (above) in Paris was built in the 12th century. It is famous for its Gothic architecture and its location on an island in the middle of the River Seine.

BELIEFS

Three-quarters of all French people are Roman Catholics, although not many of them go to church regularly, apart from at Christmas and Easter. Religion plays a smaller and smaller part in people's lives.

There are over a million Muslims and half a million Jews in our country, who each have their own religious festivals and holy days. The Jewish Sabbath lasts from sunset on Friday to sunset on Saturday. Jews worship at a temple called a synagogue.

Muslims worship at a mosque, and pray towards the east, in the direction of Mecca, their holy city. Friday is their holy day. Most French Muslims have come from North Africa. Parents in Muslim families often like their children to marry people whose parents have come from the same country, or even the same village. Young people often prefer to choose their own partner. This can cause family arguments.

France has a long Christian tradition, evident in beautiful churches and architecture, such as the nave and stained-glass window at Reims cathedral (left), where the monarchs of France were crowned.

FESTIVALS

No other country in Europe holds as many festivals as France. Some are internationally famous, such as the Cannes Film Festival, or the Mardi Gras carnival at Nice. Others are held by villages, sometimes to celebrate the harvest or patron saint. Still others celebrate local produce, such as the Bayonne Ham Fair, or the Osenbach Snail Festival.

As France is mainly Catholic, many people celebrate their saint's day. If your name is Martin, for instance, then on Saint Martin's Day, it is traditional to receive small gifts, or perhaps have a special meal.

France also has many public holidays, such as July 14, or Bastille Day. It commemorates the start of the French Revolution in 1789. The poor people rebelled against the monarchy because money was being spent on costly and unsuccessful wars. France has been a republic ever since. Today, it has a democratically-elected government.

The gypsy pilgrimage at Les Saintes-Maries-de-la-Mer (left) is a very colourful festival where relics of two Saint Marys are carried in procession to the sea. Traditional costume is worn at festivals; at Seguret (right) and at the citrus fruit festival at Menton (far right).

Minh is determined to become an architect. Her parents know that with developments in technology (left), every year there is less work for unskilled or unqualified people, particularly if they are immigrants who have recently come to France. They can face unfair treatment because they have not had the same education as other French children. Language barriers can sometimes hinder them too.

EDUCATION

In France we start school at the age of 6, although many of us attend nursery school first. Most schools in France are run by the government, but there are a few private schools. These are often run by the Catholic Church. Primary schools sometimes have classes on Saturday mornings, but then Wednesdays are usually free.

Minh will attend a primary school until the age of 11. Then, from 11 to 15, she will go to *collège*. After that, she wants to go to a *lycée*, where she will take the difficult *baccalauréat* exams which she needs to pass in order to go to university. Some of her classmates will go to special colleges instead of a *lycée* to train for specific jobs.

Minh knows that education is very important. Her grandparents fled the war in Vietnam, in the 1950s, and her parents were born in France. They would like to see their children become successful in their new country, and push them to study hard.

The University of Sorbonne (left), in Paris, is one of the oldest in the world. France is known for its intellectuals and philosophers such as Jean-Paul Sartre, and its excellence in art and literature.

INDUSTRY AND JOBS

France is one of the world's leading industrial countries. It is technologically advanced and has the world's third largest aerospace industry. The iron, steel, car and chemical industries are very important, but fewer people work in these areas than ten years ago because more jobs can be done by machines. This means that more people are working in banking, tourism, education or broadcasting. When immigrants arrive from other countries, many have to take jobs which few French people want to do, because they are low-paid, dirty or dangerous, such as street cleaning, or working in mines or on building sites. Nowadays, these jobs are disappearing, which means that unskilled immigrants may face hardship when they first arrive. Some immigrants make a living by selling their traditional food in restaurants and markets, or by running hotels.

Traditionally, the French have excelled in a number of fields, such as fashion design (left), perfumes, wine, spirits and champagne production. Wines are produced all over France, but the most famous are from Bordeaux and Burgundy (far right). True champagne only comes from the Champagne region, and the best brandy, which is also made from grapes, comes from the Cognac area.

The modern, high-tech office area shown above is a centre for business, trade and industry in Paris. Thousands of people work here everyday in the many skyscrapers.

Some foreign people make a living by running market stalls. This North African woman (above right) is selling scarves. Traditional Muslim women wear a headscarf, known as a *chador* (a sign of modesty), as part of their religion.

RURAL LIFE

Until recently, the French countryside has been relatively untouched by progress. There are modern comforts, such as electricity and telephones, but villages are still very rural. France is quite a large country, and there is still a sense of space in the countryside.

Sandrine is an Alsatian, from the Alsace region near the German border. Her village is called Kaysersberg (below left). It is in the heart of a beautiful wine-producing region and like most French villages, the pace of life is slow. The most important weekly event is market day, when the farmers sell their produce.

Although France is the leading agricultural nation in Europe, only 7 per cent of the population work on farms. This is because farms are larger and more mechanised. There are fewer opportunities for young people in rural areas today.

French farms (right) produce many things. The north and central area is suited to cereals and livestock, while the sunny south is better for fruit, and especially grapes. Vineyards are often gathered around a *château* (left and top right), a sort of grand manor house.

URBAN LIFE

More than three-quarters of our population live in cities. The biggest and most important is Paris, with a population of nine million people, followed by Lyon, Marseille, Lille, and Bordeaux, (all including suburbs).

In the cities almost everyone lives in an apartment (left), sometimes with a *concierge*, or caretaker, who looks after the building and watches who goes in and out. Some neighbourhoods, or *quartiers,* have their own character and flavour, because they are home to artists, craftspeople or immigrants. Many towns such as Périgueux (far left) and Boulogne-sur-Mer (bottom left) have open-air markets, pleasant parks to stroll in and a mixture of old buildings and new offices.

On the edge of cities are the suburbs or *banlieue.* Some of these are unattractive places to live in; flats have been badly built and are overcrowded. Many people moving from other countries live here, because they have poorly paid jobs or no job at all, and can't afford to live elsewhere.

Everyday, people commute to the city (right) from suburbs and nearby satellite towns where there is less pollution and noise, and the houses have gardens.

PARIS

Paris is the capital city of France, and its political, financial and cultural centre. It is where the president and government reside and where major policies are made. Over half the country's business is done in Paris; many companies have their headquarters here.

The city is famous for its magnificent and historic buildings, such as the Eiffel Tower, the Arc de Triomphe and the Pompidou Centre. It is also noted for its elegant *boulevards* (wide avenues), such as the Champs-Elysées, and its charming back streets.

Although Paris is not a particularly warm city out of summer, the Parisians love to be outside, where they can watch each other and be seen. There is plenty of street life, and hundreds of pavement cafés (right).

Paris is a centre of art and learning. In the past the city has attracted some of Europe's finest artists, such as Monet and Picasso. The Louvre museum houses priceless works of art, such as Leonardo da Vinci's *Mona Lisa*.

Paris is one of the world's most recognisable cities, thanks to the Eiffel Tower (right), which stands 320 m high, and the River Seine, which runs through the city centre. Tourists flock to the city to enjoy its beauty and charm.

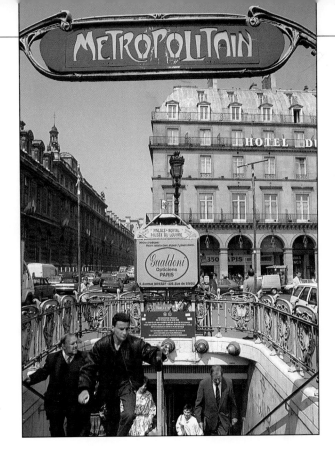

Bernard's father works at the Louvre (above). When he retires he would like to return to his village in the Dordogne, but Bernard prefers the noise and smells of the city (below), and likes travelling on the *Métro* subway (left).

SPORTS AND PASTIMES

The French love sports, especially football and cycling. The Tour de France cycle race in the summer covers around 4,800 km in three weeks, and is perhaps the toughest sporting event in the world (far right). Children and adults in all parts of France play football, and tennis and rugby are popular too.

People travel from all over France and from abroad to enjoy winter sports in the mountains. The French countryside is also ideal for activities such as climbing, hiking, canoeing or sailing.

Thierry lives in Saint-Jean-de-Luz in the French Basque country, very close to Spain. The Basques are fond of tests of strength, and his father often takes part in cart-pulling and boulder-lifting contests.

French children like to do the same as children elsewhere in Europe: go to the cinema (opposite top left) or play with our computer games or bicycles. They read a great many books of all sorts, including the comic strip, *Astérix*.

Older people enjoy less energetic activities, such as *boules* (left), a kind of bowls with heavy metal balls. A popular Algerian pastime is dominoes which they sometimes play whilst relaxing in cafés.

Thierry plays *pelote* (right), a Basque game where contestants use their fists or wicker scoops to throw the ball against the wall of the court. Above, children have fun at Futuroscope Park, a high-tech development park in Poitiers.

THE FUTURE

Like all Western countries, France has some problems to solve, such as unemployment, bad housing and pollution. For some of us, who are the children of immigrants, the old problem of racism can make us unhappy: some people treat us as foreigners, making it harder for our families to find jobs and places to live. Occasionally, racism leads to violence, although the government is trying to prevent this.

But there are also reasons for feeling confident. France is a strong supporter of a united Europe and of a single currency. Being at the heart of Europe, it is likely to benefit from these changes, which could boost trade and improve the living conditions of its population. Paris is an important city, the home of many European organisations, with major motorway links and the Channel Tunnel link with Britain.

We all like living in France. We hope that when we are adults and looking for jobs, we will have the same chances in life, and yet be proud of our own cultures.

Au revoir!

KEY FACTS

Official name: La République Française (The French Republic)

Population: 56,556,000

Area: (Including Corsica) 543,965 km^2 (209,970 miles^2)

National language: French (Regional languages and dialects include Basque, Breton, Catalan, Provençal)

Capital and largest city: Paris

Other major cities: Lyon, Marseille, Lille, Bordeaux, Toulouse, Nice

Main religions: Roman Catholic, Islam, Judaism

Ethnic groups: 93 per cent French, 7 per cent immigrants and descendants, from Algeria, Morocco, Tunisia, Italy, Portugal, Spain, Turkey, Vietnam, Niger, Cameroon and others.

Literacy : 99 per cent

Most important rivers: Loire, Seine, Rhône, Garonne

Highest mountain: Mont Blanc, 4,807 m (15,771 ft) above sea level

Climate: Generally mild, with warm summers and cool winters except for the Mediterranean coast, which is warmer all year round.

Vegetation: Fertile farmland

Major crops: Wheat, barley, sugar beet, grapes, potatoes, apples

Livestock: Poultry, cattle, sheep, goats, pigs

Manufacturing: Steel, chemicals, cars, planes, armaments, textiles

Employment: Service sector 62 per cent, manufacturing 30 per cent, agriculture and fisheries 8 per cent.

Currency: French franc

Major exports: Cars, planes, chemicals, computer equipment, plastics, iron and steel, perfumes, pharmaceutical products

Major imports: Cars, crude petroleum, natural gas, planes

INDEX

Photocredits – Abbreviations: t-top, m-middle, b-bottom, r-right, l-left
All the pictures in this book are supplied by Frank Spooner Pictures apart from the following: Front Cover tr, b, 12t, 22tr, 25tl, tr: Paul Nightingale; Cover inset, title page inset, 2-3 all, 8br, 11tl, bl, 12br, 16br, 20, 25m, 27bl, 29: Roger Vlitos; 8bl: Peter Bennett; 10, 11tr, 21t, 22tl, 27m: Charles de Vere; 11br: Eye Ubiquitous.